Adventures at the Smithsonian

Space

Courtney Acampora

Silver Dolphin

Silver Dolphin Books
An imprint of Printers Row Publishing Group
A division of Readerlink Distribution Services, LLC
10350 Barnes Canyon Road, Suite 100, San Diego, CA 92121
www.silverdolphinbooks.com

A component of ISBN 978-1-68412-601-9. Not for individual sale.

Manufactured, printed, and assembled in Shenzhen, China. HH/08/18
22 21 20 19 18   1 2 3 4 5

Written by Courtney Acampora
Designed by Dynamo Limited
Reviewed by Valerie Neal, Chair, Division of Space History
Cathleen Lewis, Aeronautics Museum Curator
Andrew K. Johnston, Geographer for the Center for Earth and Planetary Studies,
National Air and Space Museum

For Smithsonian Enterprises:
Carol LeBlanc, Senior Vice President, Education and Consumer Products
Brigid Ferraro, Vice President, Education and Consumer Products
Ellen Nanney, Licensing Manager
Kealy Gordon, Product Development Manager, Licensing

Table of Contents

What Is Space?

When you look up at the dark sky at night and see the bright, twinkly stars, you're looking at a part of space. The **universe**, or all of space, is an incredibly huge, wide-open area that holds everything that can be measured or touched. Stars, galaxies, planets, Earth, and even you, can be found in the universe!

Five hundred years ago, many people thought that the universe was like a twinkling shell surrounding Earth. Today, with the power of technology and advances in science and exploration, we're learning that space is much, much bigger! It's possible that the universe is infinite, meaning that it has no end.

Scientists measure distances across the universe in **light-years**. A light-year is the distance that light travels in one year, which is about 5.88 trillion miles. If you could travel at the speed of light, you'd be able to travel around Earth seven and a half times in one second!

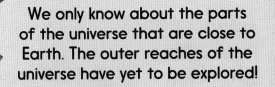

We only know about the parts of the universe that are close to Earth. The outer reaches of the universe have yet to be explored!

The universe is made up of spinning galaxies that are made up of millions of stars and systems made up of planets, comets, **asteroids**, and other space objects that **orbit** a single star. We live in a system of planets located in the Milky Way Galaxy. The Milky Way contains hundreds of billions of stars—our Sun included.

HOW OLD IS THE UNIVERSE?

Scientists are still learning what the universe is made up of and what's at the far reaches of space. Based on their findings, the universe has been measured to be 13.7 billion years old! **Astronomers** can estimate the age of the universe by studying the age of stars and measuring the rate of expansion of the universe.

Our Solar System

When you step outside during the day, one of the first things you'll notice is the Sun. It could be shining bright in the sky or hiding behind clouds. The Sun is the center of our solar system. All of the planets in our solar system revolve around it. In fact, the word "solar" means "of the Sun."

Our solar system is about 4.5 billion years old. There are eight planets in our solar system, in two groups. Four planets are **terrestrial** and four are gas giants.

Although there are thousands of stars in the night sky, only one star is in our solar system—the Sun. The Sun is so big that its **mass** causes the planets and everything else in the solar system to move in a path around it.

The solar system is always moving because the Milky Way is always rotating. The solar system travels at an average speed of 515,000 miles per hour. Even though it's moving at an incredible speed, it would take the solar system 230 million years to travel all the way around the Milky Way!

GAS GIANTS

Sun

Jupiter

Saturn

Neptune

Earth

Mars

Venus

Uranus

Mercury

TERRESTRIAL PLANETS

Moons, asteroids, and **meteors** are also part of the solar system.

Sun

The Sun is a gigantic hot star at the center of our solar system. It is so big that one million Earths could fit inside it. The Sun makes up 99.86 percent of our solar system's entire mass. It is billions of years old and will continue burning for billions of years to come.

SOLAR ERUPTIONS

A solar flare, or solar eruption, is an explosion of energy in the Sun's **atmosphere**. Sometimes, solar eruptions are so powerful they can cause spacecraft to stop working!

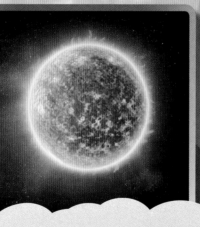

Life on Earth is possible because we are the perfect distance from the Sun—it's not too hot or too cold on Earth. It takes eight minutes for light from the Sun to reach Earth.

Mercury

Mercury is a terrestrial planet and the closest planet to the Sun. Mercury looks a lot like our Moon; it's rocky, dry, with cliffs and craters. It is also the least explored terrestrial planet.

LENGTH OF DAY: *58 Earth days, 15 hours*

LENGTH OF YEAR: *88 Earth days*

AVERAGE DISTANCE FROM THE SUN: *35,980,000 miles*

DIAMETER AT EQUATOR: *3,032 miles*

NUMBER OF MOONS: *0*

SURFACE DETAILS: *Extremely thin atmosphere, rocky terrain with ridges, cliffs, large areas that are heavily cratered, and areas that are almost crater free*

MADE OF: *Rocks and a huge iron core*

AVERAGE TEMPERATURE: *Ranges from -300°F at night to 800°F during the day*

On Mercury, the side facing the Sun is very hot while the side facing away from the Sun is close to the coldest temperatures in the solar system.

Venus

Venus is the second planet from the Sun and the closest planet from Earth. In fact, Venus and Earth are sometimes referred to as twins because they are so similar in terms of materials, size, and mass. However, there are some major differences. Venus's atmosphere is 100 times thicker than Earth's, it's much hotter, and there is no life or water.

LENGTH OF DAY: *243 Earth days*

LENGTH OF YEAR: *225 Earth days*

AVERAGE DISTANCE FROM THE SUN: *67,240,000 miles*

DIAMETER AT EQUATOR: *7,521 miles*

NUMBER OF MOONS: *0*

SURFACE DETAILS: *Hot, dry, rolling plains with some mountains and no craters*

MADE OF: *A central iron core and a rocky mantle, similar to the composition of Earth. Its atmosphere is made up of 96 percent carbon dioxide, 3 percent nitrogen, and a small amount of other gases.*

AVERAGE TEMPERATURE: *864°F*

Because of the way its clouds reflect sunlight, Venus is the brightest-looking planet in the sky from Earth.

Venus is home to Maat Mons, a massive volcano. It towers more than five and a half miles high!

Earth

We call Earth our home. The third planet from the Sun, Earth is home to more than 30 million different forms of life. From space, Earth appears blue because so much of it is covered in water. In fact, water is one of the main reasons Earth can support life.

LENGTH OF DAY: *23 hours, 56 minutes, and 4 seconds*

LENGTH OF YEAR: *365.25 days*

AVERAGE DISTANCE FROM THE SUN: *92,960,000 miles*

DIAMETER AT EQUATOR: *7,926.28*

NUMBER OF MOONS: *1*

SURFACE DETAILS: *About 70 percent is covered with water, and 30 percent is covered with rock, soil, and plants*

MADE OF: *Metals, minerals, and water*

AVERAGE TEMPERATURE: *Average of 58.2°F*

Crust

Mantle

Outer core

Inner core

THE EARTH IS MADE OF FOUR DIFFERENT LAYERS:

THE CRUST: The top layer is the layer we live on. Oceans cover about 70 percent of the surface. Earth's crust is made mostly of granite continents and basaltic rock under the oceans.

THE MANTLE: Right under the crust is a layer of very hot, dense rock called the mantle. This layer is so hot, the rock flows like liquid asphalt.

THE OUTER CORE: Earth's third layer is the outer core made of the metals nickel and iron. The outer core is so hot that these metals have melted into a liquid.

THE INNER CORE: The inner core is the Earth's center. The temperature is a whopping 9,800°F! It's so hot that the metals are squeezed together in a solid form.

Mars

Mars is the fourth planet from the Sun and is known as the "Red Planet" because its iron-rich dust has rusted. Similar to Earth, Mars has deserts, canyons, and frozen north and south poles. Scientists are particularly interested in Mars because they believe it was once more like Earth!

LENGTH OF DAY: *24 hours, 40 minutes*

LENGTH OF YEAR: *687 Earth days*

AVERAGE DISTANCE FROM THE SUN: *141,600,000 miles*

DIAMETER AT EQUATOR: *4,212 miles*

NUMBER OF MOONS: *Mars has two moons, named Phobos and Deimos.*

SURFACE DETAILS: *A rocky, solid surface that has been shaped by volcanoes, impacts from space objects, and dust storms*

MADE OF: *A core of mainly iron and sulfur and a surface of basalt and just enough iron oxide to give the planet its reddish hue*

TEMPERATURE: *High temperatures of 70°F at noon at the equator in the summer, with a low temperature of about -225°F at the poles*

Much exploration has been done on Mars. Several robotic, un-piloted spacecraft, or rovers, have landed on Mars's surface. Controlled by remote so scientists can learn more about the Red Planet, rovers move across the surface of Mars snapping photos and gathering samples.

Jupiter

Jupiter is the fifth planet from the Sun and the first of the gas giants. It is the largest planet in our solar system. Unlike Earth, which only has one moon, Jupiter holds the record of having the most moons—at least 67! Because it does not have a solid surface like the terrestrial planets, astronauts would not be able to land on Jupiter.

Jupiter is often referred to as the solar system's vacuum cleaner because its massive gravitational pull sucks in nearby comets and meteors.

LENGTH OF DAY: *10 hours*

LENGTH OF YEAR: *12 Earth years*

AVERAGE DISTANCE FROM THE SUN: *483,800,000 miles*

DIAMETER AT EQUATOR: *86,881 miles*

NUMBER OF MOONS: *At least 67*

SURFACE DETAILS: *Its atmosphere is made up of mostly hydrogen gas and helium gas, and the surface is covered in thick red, brown, yellow, and white clouds.*

MADE OF: *Mostly hydrogen and helium, with a possible molten core*

TEMPERATURE: *In the clouds of Jupiter the average temperature is -234°F, but at the planet's core it is as hot as 43,000°F, which is hotter than the surface of the Sun!*

The Great Red Spot is a massive storm that has been raging on Jupiter for more than 500 years! It once measured 25,000 miles in diameter. Now it's only a bit bigger than Earth at just under 10,000 miles in diameter!

Saturn

Saturn is one of the most recognizable planets in the solar system because of its rings. The seven ring groups are icy and made up of dust and rock pieces. Saturn is also the farthest planet that we can see from Earth with unaided eyes.

LENGTH OF DAY:
10 hours, 32 minutes

LENGTH OF YEAR:
29.5 Earth years

AVERAGE DISTANCE FROM THE SUN: *890,700,000 miles*

DIAMETER AT EQUATOR:
74,732 miles

NUMBER OF MOONS: *At least 62*

SURFACE DETAILS: *Gas*

MADE OF: *Hydrogen with lesser amounts of helium. It most likely has a thick atmosphere and a small, rocky core surrounded by a liquid.*

In 1610, Italian astronomer Galileo Galilei looked at Saturn through a telescope and noticed strange objects on each side of it, which he described as "arms." Hundreds of years later, scientists discovered that the "arms" were actually its rings!

Uranus

When viewed through a telescope, Uranus looks a bit like a glowing green pea! The methane gas in Uranus's atmosphere causes it to look blue-green. Eight times larger than Earth, Uranus is unlike any other planet in the solar system because it rotates on its side.

LENGTH OF DAY:
17.9 hours

LENGTH OF YEAR:
84.3 Earth years

AVERAGE DISTANCE FROM THE SUN:
1,787,000,000 miles

DIAMETER AT EQUATOR:
31,800 miles

NUMBER OF MOONS:
At least 27

SURFACE DETAILS:
Large, rocky core with a surface of gases and ice made of methane, hydrogen, and helium

MADE OF: *Frozen gases and a molten core. Its atmosphere is made of 83 percent hydrogen, 15 percent helium, and 2 percent methane.*

AVERAGE TEMPERATURE: *-357°F near the cloud tops*

Saturn is not the only planet in our solar system with rings—Uranus has rings, too! In 1997, scientists first spotted a band of rings around Uranus. Today, 15 rings have been discovered. Compared to Saturn, the rings around Uranus are narrow and dark.

Neptune

Neptune is the furthest planet from the Sun, so it is extremely cold. It is a deep-blue gas giant and the furthest planet ever reached by spacecraft. Neptune is an ice giant with the strongest winds in the solar system. They can reach a speed of 1,300 miles per hour!

LENGTH OF DAY:
16 hours, 6 minutes

LENGTH OF YEAR:
164.79 Earth years

AVERAGE DISTANCE FROM THE SUN: *28 billion miles*

DIAMETER AT EQUATOR:
30,599 miles

NUMBER OF MOONS: *At least 14*

SURFACE DETAILS: *Gases*

MADE OF: *Very cold hydrogen, helium, methane gases, and ice with a rocky core*

AVERAGE TEMPERATURE: *-353°F*

Since it was discovered in 1846, Neptune has completed only one orbit around the Sun!

Scientists have found evidence that there might be diamonds on Neptune. The high pressure on Neptune could be strong enough to squeeze the carbon on the planet into diamonds!

Stars

Although stars appear to us as tiny pinpricks of light in the night sky, they are actually enormous! Stars are hot, brightly burning balls of gas that burn for billions of years. On Earth, the closest star is the Sun.

Although our solar system orbits around one star, there can be billions of stars in one galaxy and there may be hundreds of billions of galaxies in the universe! There are many different kinds of stars, varying in brightness, color, mass, and size.

Groups of bright stars in our sky seem to form patterns and shapes. If you connect the bright dots with imaginary lines you can see shapes that look like people and animals. These patterns are called **constellations**.

Asteroids
and Icy Worlds

Asteroids are leftovers from planets. They are made of iron and rock, and orbit the Sun like planets do. Our solar system is home to millions of asteroids. Most of them orbit the Sun in an asteroid belt between Mars and Jupiter. The largest asteroid is Ceres.

Comets also orbit the Sun, but they are made of ice and rock and have visible tails when they approach the Sun.

When an asteroid crashes into a planet, it creates an impact crater. Asteroids caused the craters on Earth's Moon. There aren't too many craters on Earth because our atmosphere causes asteroids to burn up before they can reach Earth's surface.

A meteoroid is a small piece of space rubble. When a meteoroid enters Earth's atmosphere, it heats up and glows, becoming a meteor. If the meteor doesn't burn out before hitting Earth, it's called a meteorite.

When you wish upon a shooting star, you're really wishing upon a meteor!

KUIPER BELT

Beyond the planet Neptune lies a region full of icy bodies, including the dwarf planet Pluto. The hundreds and thousands of ice bodies in the Kuiper Belt can be larger than 62 miles across! In 1992, the first Kuiper Belt object was discovered. *New Horizons* was the first spacecraft to explore the Kuiper Belt.

New Horizons image of Pluto and Charon, Pluto's largest moon.

Earth's Moon

Moons are natural objects that orbit planets, thanks to gravity. Some planets, like Jupiter, have many moons, and some, like Earth, only have one. Astronomers believe that a very long time ago, Earth smashed into an object the size of Mars. The collision broke off huge chunks of Earth that were flung into space. Over time the Earth chunks joined and made our Moon.

LENGTH OF DAY: *29.5 Earth days*

LENGTH OF YEAR: *27 Earth days*

AVERAGE DISTANCE FROM EARTH: *238,900 miles*

DIAMETER AT EQUATOR: *2,159 miles*

SURFACE DETAILS: *Rocky, with hills, mountains, and craters*

MADE OF: *The crust is made mostly of volcanic material. The small core may be metallic iron, sulfur, and nickel.*

TEMPERATURE: *-243°F to 253°F*

If you were to travel to the Moon today, you'd see the footprints of the first astronauts to land there in 1969. That's because there is no weathering from wind or rain, so they will still be on the Moon's surface millions of years from now.

When you look up at the Moon at night, you'll notice dark spots covering its surface. Those spots, which we now know are darker areas covered by volcanic rock, were once called "seas." Unlike Earth, the Moon doesn't have an atmosphere to protect it, so meteors and asteroids crash into the Moon, leaving huge craters.

Our Moon may be smaller than Earth, but it still has a strong gravitational pull that is powerful enough to create ocean tides. As the Moon revolves around our planet, Earth and the water on the side of Earth nearest the Moon are pulled by the Moon's gravity, creating a tidal bulge or high tide. The surrounding water is also pulled toward this bulge. Although Earth is entirely pulled by the Moon's gravity, the water on the opposite side of Earth is not affected by the pull. The water then creates a high tide on the other side of the planet.

Space Exploration

Humans have been staring up at the stars and planets since they first walked on Earth. It wasn't until the last 500 years that the first astronomer proposed that the Earth rotated and revolved around the Sun; before that it was widely believed that everything in the universe circled around us. It was only in 1961 that the first human was sent into space to orbit the Earth, and only from 1969 to 1972 that humans went to the Moon. Space explorers venturing out to the planets have all been robots. Today, we are creating and using new technologies to learn more about the far reaches of the universe.

HUBBLE SPACE TELESCOPE

In 1990, NASA launched one of the most powerful telescopes yet—the Hubble Space Telescope. Unlike telescopes on the ground, the Hubble Space Telescope orbits above Earth's atmosphere. Its astonishingly clear views of the universe have transformed our understanding of outer space.

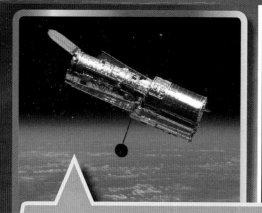

The Hubble Space Telescope is famous for snapping stunning photos of distant planets, stars, nebulae, and galaxies. The Hubble Space Telescope orbits Earth at a speed of 17,500 miles per hour. Since it was launched, it has collected more than 570,000 images.

VOYAGER

The twin Voyager spacecraft explored the gas giant planets, then traveled beyond the orbits of the planets of our solar system. Both *Voyager 1* and *Voyager 2* were launched in 1977 to explore the outer planets. After discovering active volcanoes on Jupiter's moon Io and learning about the rings of Saturn, their mission was extended.

MARS ROVER

In 2003, two Mars rovers were sent to land on Mars: *Spirit* and *Opportunity*. *Spirit* explored Mars until 2010, and *Opportunity* was still going in 2016, with its end date not yet known. These two small rovers made the major discovery that Mars has signs that liquid water once was on its surface.

Martian rovers are robotic and equipped with cameras and a variety of tools and instruments for exploring. A robotic arm uses instruments to examine soil and rocks the way a geologist would.

Curiosity is a ten-foot-long, six-wheeled robot that landed on Mars in 2012. While exploring Mars's surface and gathering samples, *Curiosity* hopes to discover if there was ever life on Mars or if life on Mars could ever be possible.

Inside a Spacesuit

Spacesuits are much more than a cool uniform astronauts wear on missions. A spacesuit is more like a personal spacecraft! Spacesuits allow astronauts to work under the extreme conditions in space—scorching and freezing temperatures, lack of air pressure, radiation, and small high-speed debris! Spacesuits also provide astronauts with oxygen and water.

Astronauts are people trained to travel in space. They ride in capsules on top of rockets or, for many years, went in a rocket-launched space shuttle that looked like an airplane. In 1958, the U.S. Congress created the National Aeronautics and Space Administration (NASA). For more than fifty years, NASA has trained astronauts to go to the Moon, live in space near Earth for long periods of time, and has used technology to learn more about the universe.

Some spacesuits were connected to spacecraft via an umbilical cord lifeline when astronauts did not need to go far from the spacecraft cabin. The Apollo, shuttle, and space station suits were fitted with their own life-support system, a backpack, that allowed astronauts to explore away from the lunar module.

Spacesuits are white because white reflects heat. In space, temperatures can be over 275°F!

The helmet is designed to protect the astronaut's head. A visor covered with a thin layer of gold can be pulled down like sunglasses to block the Sun's harmful rays.

The suit's backpack holds the oxygen the astronaut breathes and removes carbon dioxide that the astronaut exhales.

Specially made for the Apollo missions, flexible gloves were designed for holding instruments, gathering rock and soil samples, and conducting tests.

PGA 076

APOLLO 11

CDR

This spacesuit was worn by astronaut Neil Armstrong, the first man to walk on the Moon. Armstrong wore this spacesuit during the Apollo 11 mission in 1969.

Apollo mission suits differ from other spacesuits because astronauts had to walk on the rocky and dusty surface of the Moon. These special boots were designed for walking on a rocky surface.

Life in Space

Astronauts must train and prepare for life in space because they feel much lighter there. In space, astronauts can't walk on the ground like they do on Earth. Instead, they float!

It's important to exercise on Earth, but it's even more important to exercise in space. Typically, astronauts exercise for two hours every day because they lose muscle mass faster in space.

CHEWING GUM

PEACHES
3 oz. cold water
15-20 minutes

Astronauts in space enjoy their favorite foods like they do on Earth. Food is prepared and packaged differently, to avoid crumbs and to last longer, because there is no refrigerator. Whether it's shrimp or macaroni and cheese, astronauts can eat almost anything in space. Salt and pepper, however, are in liquid form because the small grains would float away.

Astronauts spend their days working so it's important that they get plenty of rest. Since they are weightless, astronauts can sleep in many positions in space. To avoid floating around and bumping into something, they zip themselves up in a sleeping bag that's secured to a wall.

Astronauts in space have the same hygiene routines as they do on Earth. They shower, brush their teeth, shave, and go to the bathroom. When showering, astronauts use a waterless shampoo. Astronauts bring a personal hygiene kit that contains their favorite items. They use a toilet without water; it works more like a vacuum cleaner!

Apollo 11 Mission

In the 1960s, two nations set their sights on racing to the Moon: the United States and the Soviet Union. The Soviet program was unsuccessful, but the American program led to humans walking on the Moon. The three astronauts, Neil Armstrong, Buzz Aldrin, and Michael Collins, would perform scientific experiments on the Moon's surface, take photographs of the lunar terrain, and bring soil and rock samples back to Earth. On July 16, 1969, at the Kennedy Space Center in Florida, Apollo 11 and its three-man crew blasted off from Earth and headed to the Moon.

It took the astronauts three days to finally arrive on the Moon. On July 20, 1969, Americans Neil Armstrong and Buzz Aldrin became the first humans to set foot on the Moon. Michael Collins remained alone in orbit around the Moon until Armstrong and Aldrin rejoined him for the trip home.

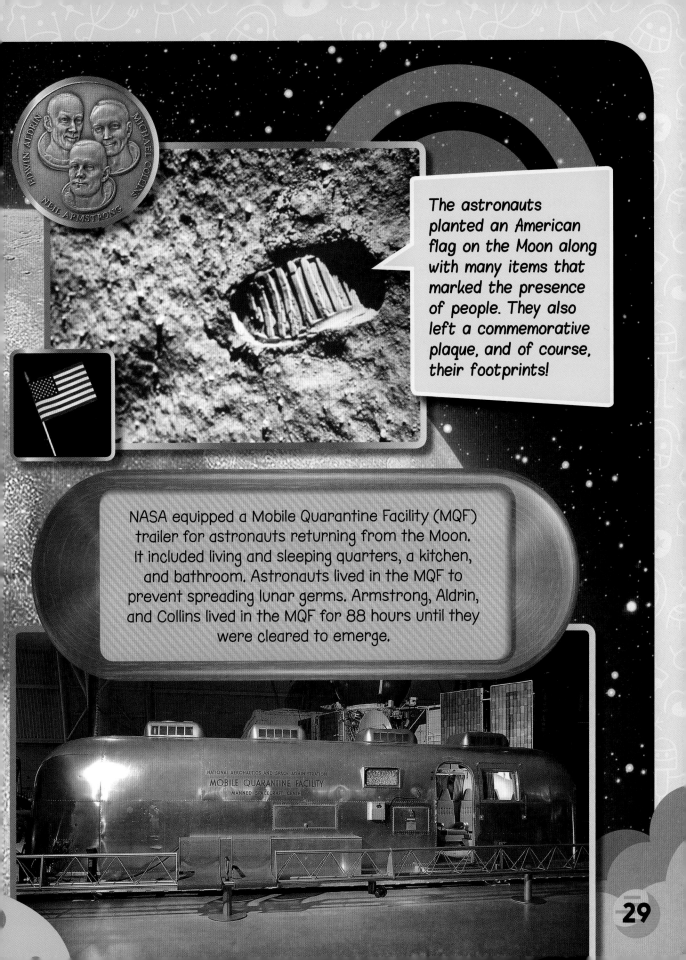

The astronauts planted an American flag on the Moon along with many items that marked the presence of people. They also left a commemorative plaque, and of course, their footprints!

NASA equipped a Mobile Quarantine Facility (MQF) trailer for astronauts returning from the Moon. It included living and sleeping quarters, a kitchen, and bathroom. Astronauts lived in the MQF to prevent spreading lunar germs. Armstrong, Aldrin, and Collins lived in the MQF for 88 hours until they were cleared to emerge.

Spacecraft

Right now there are spacecraft snapping photos, collecting data, and conducting tests, further illuminating the mysteries of our solar system and beyond. Since the 1960s, a variety of different spacecraft have been sent into space; some of them extend the range of what astronauts can do there.

The *Cassini-Huygens* Spacecraft is a joint effort between NASA, the European Space Agency, and Italian Space Agency. It consists of an array of powerful instruments and cameras. The *Cassini* was launched in 1997, and reached its destination, Saturn, in 2004. Since then, it has orbited the gas giant, taking amazing photos of Saturn's rings, moons, and weather.

Image of Saturn from the *Cassini*

The Apollo 15, 16, and 17 lunar missions included a Lunar Roving Vehicle (LRV). It was a battery-powered "dune buggy" used to explore the Moon's surface. It carried tools, gear, rock and soil samples and, of course, astronauts!

In order to fit inside the lunar module, the LRV was folded up into a small package and then was unfolded for use. The battery-powered LRV could drive around for 78 hours, allowing astronauts to roam away from their lander to investigate nearby hills, craters, and other interesting features on the Moon.

ORBITERS

Orbiters have played a vital role in space exploration—they transport astronauts to and from space. Although no longer in service, space shuttles *Atlantis*, *Discovery*, *Endeavour*, *Columbia*, and *Challenger* paved the way for the possibilities of space exploration.

Space Shuttle *Discovery*

In 1984, the space shuttle *Discovery* launched into space. Until 2011, when the space program ended, *Discovery* flew more missions than any other space shuttle—flying 39 times! *Discovery* has played an important role in space exploration. In 1990, the Hubble Space Telescope was launched from *Discovery*. From the *Discovery's* windows and cargo bay, stunning photos of Earth have been captured.

QUICK FACTS ABOUT *DISCOVERY*:

★ *Spent 365 days in space*

★ *Held a record-setting total crew of 251*

★ *First U.S. space shuttle to visit Mir, a Russian space station, in 1995*

★ *Flown by the first female space shuttle pilot and two female shuttle commanders*

★ *Named after two famous sailing ships from the 1600s*

In 2008, the crew aboard *Discovery* brought a Buzz Lightyear toy to the International Space Station (ISS). He lived on the ISS until 2009 when the *Discovery* brought him back to Earth.

Discovery missions transported astronauts, launched important satellites, and helped build the International Space Station.

On April 17, 2012, *Discovery* flew on the back of a specially-designed airliner over Washington, D.C., and landed at Washington-Dulles International airport. Two days later, it was parked inside the Smithsonian National Air and Space Museum, where visitors can marvel at its size and its 150-million-mile journey through space.

International
Space Station

A space station is a home and workplace that remains in low orbit around Earth for a long time. Space stations allow scientists to study many things in weightlessness or microgravity, including the effects of long-term spaceflight on the human body.

First launched in 1998 with many modules added over the years, the International Space Station (ISS) was built so that astronauts from all over the world could visit and learn about space. Its crew spends 35 hours a week conducting research, advancing knowledge about Earth and space. The ISS is so large and reflective that it can often be seen from Earth with unaided eyes.

Traveling 17,500 miles per hour, the ISS circles the globe every 90 minutes, seeing 15 or 16 sunrises and sunsets each day. It cost 100 billion dollars to build the ISS. Portions of the ISS were brought up into space one by one, mostly by space shuttle, and astronauts gradually assembled it—like a puzzle.

The International Space Station is the largest man-made object in space, an engineering marvel. It is as large as a football field and almost as long as the National Air and Space Museum. Research performed on the ISS has set the stage for what it's like to live in space and what lies ahead in the expansive universe.

NASA can send you a text message or email letting you know when the ISS will fly over your area so you can step outside and see it!

Glossary

Asteroids: small, rocky and metallic bodies that orbit the Sun

Astronauts: people who are trained to live, work, and travel in spacecraft in outer space

Astronomers: people who study stars, planets, comets, and asteroids

Atmosphere: the layer of gases surrounding a planet or moon

Constellations: recognizable patterns of a group of stars

Craters: large, circular impressions caused by meteorite impacts on the surface of a planet or moon

Galaxies: massive groups of stars, planets, gas, and dust

Gravity: the force of attraction between objects that depends on their mass

Light-years: units of distance that light travels in one year (5.88 trillion miles)

Mass: the amount of matter in an object

Meteors: "falling stars," small rocky or metallic bodies from outer space that glow from the heat as they streak through Earth's atmosphere

Orbit: the path of a planet, moon, comet, or spacecraft around another body, such as a planet, moon, or star

Terrestrial: of, on, or relating to land

Universe: all the space, matter, and energy in existence

Solar System: a group of planets, asteroids, comets, and moons that orbit a star. Our solar system is made up of eight planets (Mercury, Venus, Earth, Mars, Jupiter, Saturn, Uranus, and Neptune) and their moons, as well as asteroids and comets that orbit the Sun

3-D Model Instructions

Complete one model at a time. Press out the pieces and arrange them as shown. Using the numbers on the pictures here, match the slots and assemble your 3-D space vehicles.

Lunar Roving Vehicle

The battery-powered LRV could drive around for 78 hours, allowing astronauts to roam away from their lander to investigate nearby hills, craters, and other interesting features on the Moon.

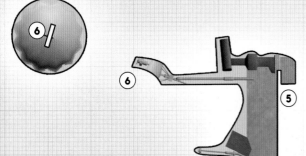

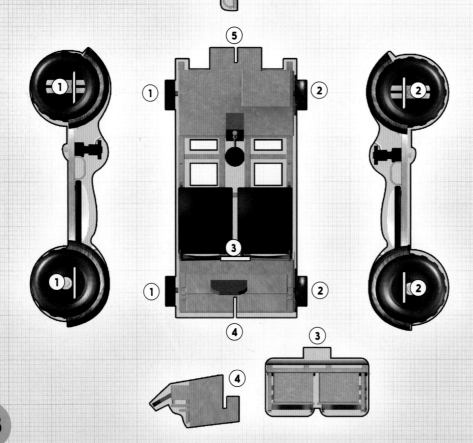

International Space Station

The International Space Station (ISS) was built so that astronauts from all over the world could visit and learn about space. It is the largest man-made object in space.

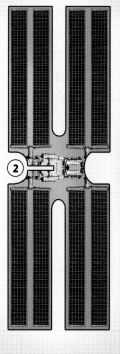

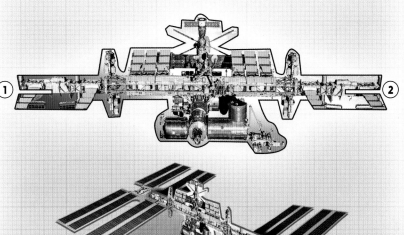

Mars Rover

Controlled by remote so scientists can learn more about the Red Planet, rovers move across the surface of Mars, snapping photos and gathering samples.

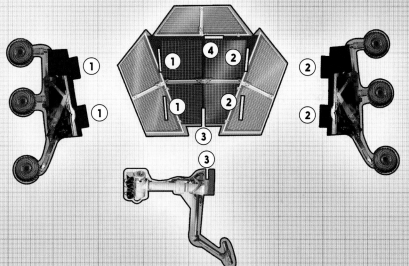

Diorama Instructions

Bring your own space scene to life by building a dramatic diorama. It's easy!

1. The inside of the box lid and base will be the walls of your diorama. The unfolding board will be the ground. Decorate these with reusable stickers as desired.

2. Press out the stand-up pieces and fold each as shown, then put aside.

3. Stand the box lid and base upright and at an angle as shown. Lay the angled back edges of the floor piece on top of the box sides. Now arrange your stand-up pieces the way you want on the moon surface.

4. Change the moon to Mars, using the other side of the unfolding board, and the matching press-out piece as shown.

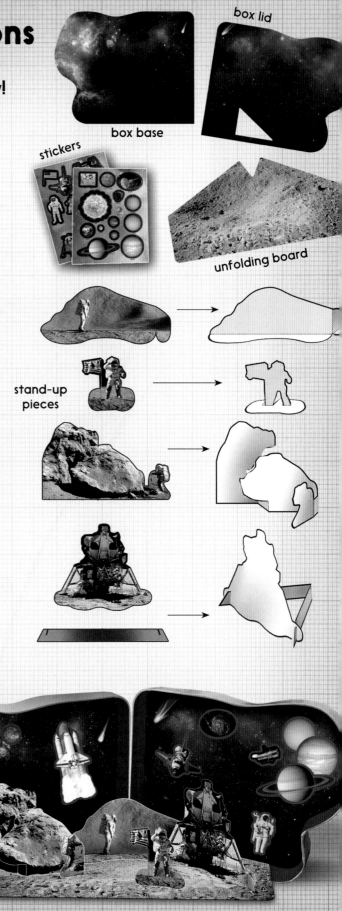

box lid

box base

stickers

unfolding board

stand-up pieces